A Beginners Guide to
Analog (film) Photography.

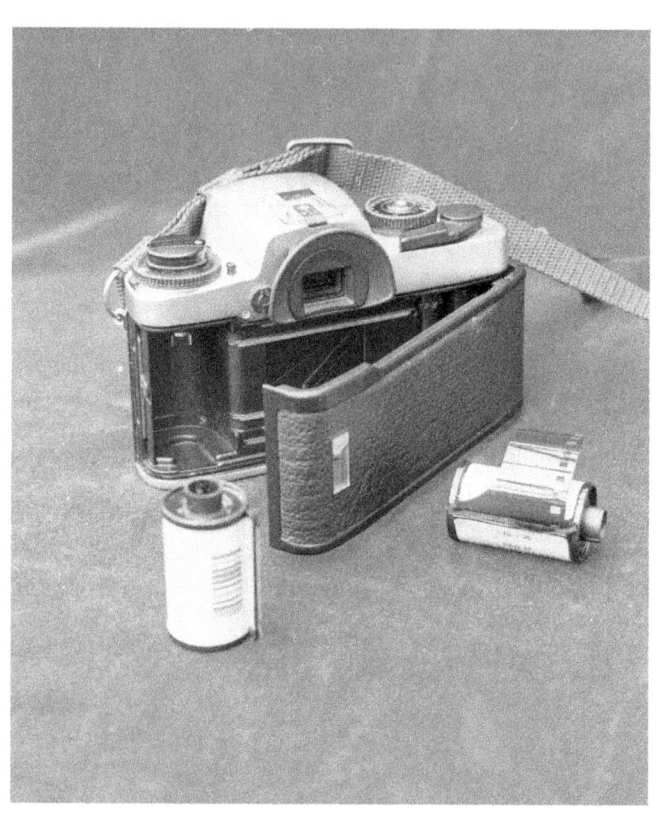

A Beginners Guide to Analog (film) Photography.

John A Plowman

König Books UK
Whoever Thinks.. Reads Books
König Publishing
2018

Copyright

First Printing: December 2018

ISBN: 978-0-244-73946-1

König Publishing
115 Loughborough Road
HATHERN, Leicestershire, LE12 5HZ

www.konigbooks.uk

Ordering Information:
Trade discounts are available on quantity purchases by Booksellers, Camera Clubs and Associations, Schools & Colleges and Adult Education Sector. For details, contact the publisher at the above listed address.

U.S. trade bookstores and wholesalers: Please contact Konig Publishing at Tel: +44 773 773 8018 or email sales@konigbooks.uk

Contents

Introduction

The Reason for writing this book

It was August, it was hot, and after a search for marine interest at a popular seaside town, I was sitting in front of a well-earned coffee, at one of the local cafes.

It was quite busy, full of trippers, and opposite me, a couple with a youngster in a push chair.

Nearing the end of my coffee, I nodded to the mother and inquired of the youngsters age. "Just a little over two years" was the reply. "He watches every movement and is into everything" "That is to be expected at that age" I replied, and reaching into my wallet, produced a photograph of my Daughter Veronica.

"This is my daughter" I explained, "perhaps a year or two older, - she was fascinated by the action of a hand driven coffee grinder and would not leave it alone" There was a quick look in my direction, and then the smiling comment "You mean your Granddaughter?" "Oh no, I corrected, *My daughter.* She was 61 in February this year, (pause) I use film you see."

Another look at the snap, and then a meaningful look at her husband. Just one word "Bill?" but it was full of meaning. Nothing more was said. I was convinced that couple will shortly be making a certain purchase.

Returning home after that little chat in the Cafe', I felt intuitively there was a widespread need for a little basic guidance, not perhaps for the enthusiasts, but the average person, in order that the advantages and permanence of Film Photography could be grasped.

Thus, this little booklet came into being, hopefully to bring joy and understanding to one and all.

Why film?

Film photography, or rather pompously "analogue" photography, is based on chemistry. Good, old fashioned *permanent* chemistry. It was devised by one of the great people in our history, and those wishing to investigate, can call up Wikipedia, and feed in the magic name "Scott Talbot".

After considerable experiments, Scott Talbot had found that certain chemicals reacted to the effects of light. We all know what followed, and photography was born. Scott Talbot coated glass plates with this new substance, known these days as "emulsion".

With several technical contributions from the French, the new science quickly established itself, and became an industry in its own right. Television was yet to be devised, the transistor was not discovered until 1935, so film photography was the pinnacle of innovation.

Photographs captured on glass plates, could be printed with ease, and duplicates sold to an enthusiastic Public. The advances seemed natural, for *Nature* is analogue.

Progress was steady, and the unwieldy glass plates eventually became replaced with cut film, initially the same size as the plate, but made from cellulose acetate. Eastman Kodak jumped on the band wagon, and soon we were flooded with the box camera, then the folding camera for the pocket.

The cut film was reduced in size, and made up into rolls, and sold in light proof reels to fit the new cameras. The film industry was not far behind, and a new thriving industry, the "movie" arrived. This used a film format even smaller, and it was provided with sprocket holes to pick up the gears in the new (hand cranked) movie cameras.

In the 1920's a German optical Engineer Oscar Barnack (working for the firm Ernst Leitz. Wetzlar) decided to take a dramatic step and devise a pocket camera that could use cine' film.

There was scientific outrage that such a daring move should be made, for such a device would require a lens of such outstanding quality that it did not exist. However, the application of outstanding genius on his part produced such a lens, and the Leica Camera was born.

Today, cameras all over the World are using cine' film, now generally known as "35mm", and Leica still hold a prestigious position although after world war two Japan was quickly on the scene, and names like Nikon and Pentax, but also Carl Zeiss in Germany became names to be reckoned with.

To this day, some important security data is still stored on micro film, (microfiche) demonstrating the reliability, security, and permanence of film as an invincible and private store of data. It is interesting to note that analog film images may be copyrighted and used in court, whereas digital images may not.

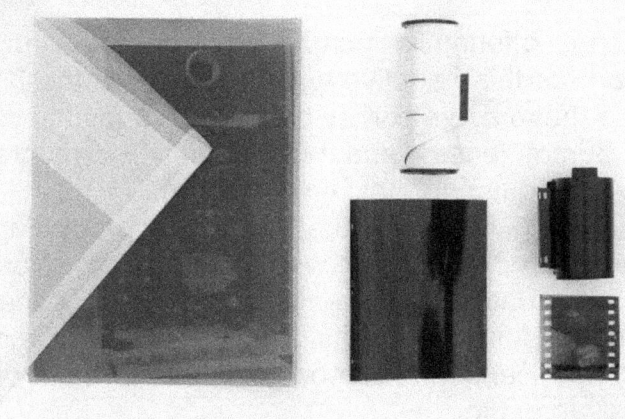

Film formats over the years; far from subtle! Left: Half plate (originally glass but cut film and storage bag shown) Centre; the popular 120 roll film, and Right; the widely used 35mm cassette, and one frame shown.

The half plate format is still widely used in some professional circles, although most now have gone over to the 5"X4" standard. There are one or two startling exceptions to this, typically the World-renowned Ansell Adams uses 10"X8" plates, so, with high performance lenses, the amount of detail stored in one of these would be "Terra pixel" in modern parlance.

The ever popular 120 roll film has maintained a significant presence to-day. The roll, being 6cm wide, thus one dimension is already fixed. Kodak brought out many pocket "folders", producing a 6cm X 9cm negative.

In the interests of economy, encouraged by several manufacturers, a new masking appeared, providing a 6cm square picture. This was popular, as it meant it was no longer necessary to twist the camera to suit the subject.

There was a further stage in this reduction technique of the "Medium Format" (to name it correctly) and cameras were appearing, offering a 6cmX2,5cm negative. In the writer's opinion, as this negative was barely twice the 35mm full format size these seem somewhat pointless, as the range of precision 35mm lenses and high definition film are so plentiful, they can "outshoot" this tiny MF format.

It is refreshing to note that a large proportion of professionals using MF, do so with a 6cmX7cm. Format, promoted it is suspected by Mamiya. This is an excellent format, capable of stunning results, for the Company produce both an SLR and Rangefinder models in this format, with a range of lenses to die for.

The 35mm format has been the subject of experimentation over the years. In the 1930's a German "Robot" camera was produced.

This had a wind-up clockwork mechanism, and it enabled photographs to be taken in quick succession, as wind on was powered and automatic.

The format was reduced from the standard 24mm X 36mm to 24mm square, presumably to reduce the transit time between frames. Although providing proportionally more shots per roll, the idea never really caught on in the UK.

Even the standard 35mm format has been reviewed by the "Half frame" enthusiasts, encouraged by a rather smart and tiny pocket camera by Rollei of Germany.

The concept was flawed in the writer's opinion by the difficulty in producing really big enlargements, and the initial enthusiasm withered away. The standard 24mmX36mm format is firmly established.

Painting with light.

Working on the premise that one does not need to know how an engine works in order to drive a car, we come to the "opt out" clause, for (hopefully) a small number of happy snappers who will be quite content to take their pictures with careless abandon, knowing however, that what they have taken is secure and safe, sitting in their pocket, and not somewhere "in the clouds". Fully automatic film cameras do exist, and these are discussed briefly later in the book.

We can readily get into a non-technical simile of camera techniques, by using a simple analogy:

We have a wine glass, which is going to be our picture, for it is really the emulsion on the film.

We have a bottle, full of wine, which is the light source.

Stuck in the top of the wine glass we have rather a clever funnel, with adjustments let into the stem. Without adjustment, the glass is quite empty, and will remain so without intervention.

There are two clever adjustments in the funnel stem, and these are adjusted by the user.

These adjusters can be named and come one below the other in no particular order. The first is the lens of course, for our scene must be recorded. The adjuster here is called *The Iris,* a name to remember when the camera is on our lap. The other adjuster, (an on/off tap) which does a vital job, is called *the shutter.*

Remember, we must fill the glass between them to get a picture. As one turns the Iris adjuster, the hole through the funnel becomes wider or narrower, depending on the setting. On the other hand, the shutter is spring loaded, and does not wish to be open at all.

By means of clever mechanical tricks however it can be persuaded to open for just a moment, at some selected setting chosen by the user. There is a subtle interaction between the Iris and the Shutter, both wishing to ensure that the glass is filled.

By opening the Iris quite wide, the glass will fill quickly, and the shutter only needs to open very briefly. Should the iris aperture be set small, then the dwell time on the shutter needs to be longer, but what to set? Obviously to shoot something moving, a short shutter speed is needed, and various combinations must be considered.

Look back to the old "movie" days of the 1930's when the film Director would rush around with his baseball cap on back to front, and a little black box around his neck. This was an *Exposure Meter*, and it was not long before this device was miniaturized and fitted into the camera, suggesting optimal combinations of settings, merely by pressing a button.

One last vital and variable parameter, and that is film speed, which must be set into our mix, but here the camera manufacturers have come to our rescue and have fitted little electrical fingers inside the compartment holding the film.

These pick up a code on the outside of the film cassette, and automatically feed the data into the camera. Not available to all but look for the abbreviation "DX coded" as this defines the facility. If this is not available, there will obviously be a means of entering the film speed manually.

Defining a camera.

We now have all the parts, we can identify the position of the film, with its all-important emulsion, then the lens with its adjustable Iris, and the adjustable shutter, sometimes in the lens (Compur type), or adjacent in the body.

Standing on the shelf, a lens is usually defined by its focal length, then after the "slash", a figure related to the optical diameter, when fully open. This is referred to as "full aperture", or perhaps "full stop".

The markings for the iris of the lens may seem confusing at first, but they relate to the area of the lens opening and not the diameter. These various positions are called "*stops*" so one click is one stop.

Note that closing-down from say f/2, just one stop, halves the working *area* and not the diameter, so this move does not indicate f/4, but as we are working in areas, so, halving the area indicates f/2.8, and is correctly marked thus.

Do not worry about the math's, just remember that one click-stop either way is changing the *active area* of the lens by half or twice as appropriate. The fundamental understanding of *stops* is not vital but is quickly picked up after a week or so "in the field".

The essential thing to remember, is that one stop-change on the iris appropriately halves or doubles the lens sensitivity, and will require an harmonious change in the shutter speed to accord.

The shutter speed increments, however, are quite easily understood, and usually halve, as one works around the scale. Most cameras will go down to one second, and "up" to 1/1000 sec.

To obtain a shutter opening of more than one second, a position marked "B" will be provided. Here, the shutter will remain open as long as the release is pressed. Obviously both a tripod and a *cable release* are required for this manoeuvre.

Take the first step with care, for the first tryout, it is not necessary to spend a lot of money. To start with, it is not vital to find a camera with interchangeable lenses.

A simple fixed lens will do at first, and it surprising what can be found, not in the eager dealers' front window, but snuggled away in the various charity shops scattered about the country. The range of prices for a simple film camera are staggering, hence my urgent appeal to visit charity shops for a good browse around.

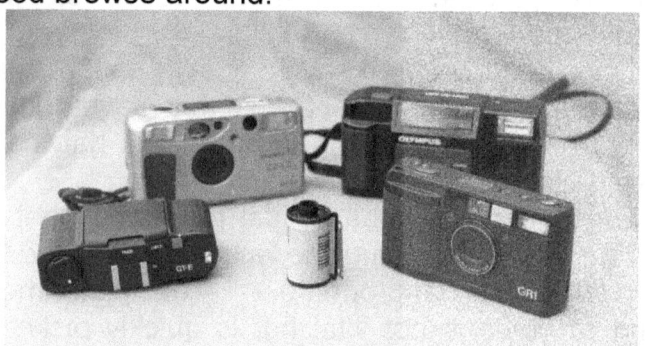

My favourite pocket camera, the 28mm /2.8 Ricoh GR3(right) is the one I always carry in my back pocket, seldom needed of course, but always there in a situation. This camera had the advantage that it would record the date of the taking, a valuable tool in today's World. It failed me!

The computer chip failed, and it was not replaceable, and thus a write off. Determined to replace it, I was horrified to see one advertised at £300 second hand. Patience prevailed, and I picked one up for £50.

Another little Gem is the Minox GT-E, (left) a name to recall, for it is the 35mm equivalent to the James Bond miniature spy camera. A 35mm f/2.8 lens, but the front folds up, and the whole thing is little bigger than twenty cigarettes.

It was described in the Amateur Photographer as "The camera for the enthusiast who knows what he is about" unfair really, for once the iris is set manually, the internal exposure meter will adjust the shutter speed to suit. Perhaps the magazine is referring to adjusting the focus using a distance scale on the lens housing, and not your eye in the viewfinder!

At one time, the Yashica-T (known as the "Eagle Eye") (centre left) was very popular and retailed new at £105. Using a 35mm f/2.8 lens as in the Minox, the Yashica did not fold, and accordingly was somewhat fatter. A sharp lens however, and the camera has an unusual advantage that it had a right-angle finder option.

This meant that held inverted over the head, one could still compose pictures over the obstructions in front of you. They must have sold hundreds on this aspect alone. A good starter, and much easier to find than a Minox.

Last, but by no means least in this short list of second handers, is the "Olympus Trip". (centre right of previous picture) Olympus made over a *million* of these, and most charity shops are full of them. Various models were produced offering a range of advantages, and they even used the easy to get ordinary torch batteries.

An illustration of all four of these "Starter" cameras is below.

Beginners Guide to Analog (film) Photography

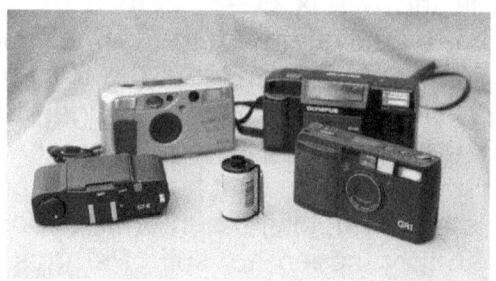

(Note: few second-hand cameras are supplied with an instruction leaflet, but OTC Ltd can usually supply these quite swiftly.)

Moving up. The SLR and the Rangefinder.

Imbued with the joy of 35mm photography, it is easy to envisage the versatility of a camera with an interchangeable lens facility.

Great names in the field of SLR (single lens reflex) are everywhere, and typically at the Farnborough Air Display, one could see an absolute sea of telephoto lenses swaying skywards in perfect unison like straw in the wind, whilst following the aircraft. A very powerful sight

Whether we go for the SLR or rangefinder type, needs considerable thought. The design of the SLR hinged on the design of the pentaprism, and its ability to produce an image before the eye, that was erect (not inverted) and right handed.

Usually, on the screen provided for the pentaprism there would be fitted a ring of microprisms, that indicate by their clarity that you are in focus.

This mechanism is not so easy to grasp for a beginner to the system, and in fact the configuration of the readout will vary from make to make.

A two-minute training period with a sheet of newspaper will suffice. Open a page upon the floor, and stand over it at a distance of, say 3-4 feet.

If your camera is manual, select "full aperture", (automatics will have already done this for you). Viewing in the finder, swing the focus ring wildly from either side. At the two extremes the image will just be a tangled mess.

Come back slowly and note the image will change in size and become clearer. Note two concentric circles in the centre of the picture. The area inside the smaller area is clear.

The "frothy" area between the two rings are the microprisms. Slowly twist the focus, and note that the general area clears, as do the microprisms.

Now move the camera over to an edge, or perhaps a vertical border, and see-saw the focus. The tiny circular area in the central portion will split into two parts moving away from one another in conjunction with your adjustment.

Once the two halves of the vertical edge are aligned, then focus is perfect. In the field, almost anything can be used, say a medal ribbon, or suit lapel. In the unlikely situation that your subject does not have a single edge, then concentrate on the microprisms. When in focus, these become completely clear.

The rangefinder camera works on a different principle, there are two mirrors, but more recently, a fixed mirror and a prism, the latter sitting on a rotating platform, coupled to an arm carrying a tiny roller that picks up a cam on the back of the lens.

The two contributing elements are set apart as wide as possible, as this increases accuracy. The optical arrangement will insert, in the centre of the viewfinder, a second image, quite small and centrally placed. We now have two images, the real and the contrived from the rangefinder.

By turning the lens, (and of course, the cam) until the two images coincide, the lens is in focus. Rangefinders are much easier to use, and immensely accurate, for the principle is used for rangefinder guidance in Artillery. However, rangefinder cameras are much more difficult to find than the SLR type.

As with 35mm starter type cameras, removable lens camera bodies will show a staggering range of asking prices, and extreme caution is vital. Private purchase is often safer, and an advertisement in a *local* paper or magazine can be helpful.

It is vital that you have a chance to examine the camera, for detectable wear on the pressure plate (where it guides the film) means excessive use.

Regrettably, many cameras are ruined not by use, but neglect. Typically, a grieving widow might bring a loved one's camera to sell, but on opening, discover that the batteries had been left in for several years, and are sitting in a cavity choked with corrosion.

The batteries are not always the culprit, I have seen a good camera utterly ruined by mildew! -It had been left in damp conditions for about six months!

As to be expected, the choice of which body to choose is really dictated by the number of dedicated lenses that are available for the body you are considering.

Of course, several optical firms produced "uncommitted" lenses that are offered with an adapter at the interface, so that they can be fitted to most of the popular makes of camera.

Whilst a good idea in concept, with one or two remarkable exceptions, they cause disappointment, and are best avoided.

Nikon for one, made capital of this, and suggested to customers that they should avoid fitting a "bottle bottom" to their Nikon body. Most enthusiasts realise whom they were getting at.

What is available? Finding something suitable

Those unable to satisfy the need for instant satisfaction will be pleased to know that there is now a choice of "instant cameras" that will produce, in just a few moments, a credit card sized print that can be handled straight away.

These are all of fairly recent new design, and unlikely to be available second hand. Furthermore, the films made for them are unlikely to fit the old "Polaroid Land" cameras, so no possible short cuts here.

The archival permanence of these prints is not known. Of this new group, the Fuji Instax mini 90 is probably the best value for money, but choose wisely, for even Leica are now on the scene in this connection.

Using the regular films, we can start with the "no thinking required", a fully automatic camera. There is an aspect of this that may attract, but it must be remembered that the higher the complexity, the more likelihood of a shorter working life.

With the fully automatic camera, provided the user can master loading the film, the rest is entirely in the hands of the internal wizardry.

The shutter setting, lens *stops,* and even focus, is left to the internals. A technically perfect picture may result, but only in the terms of the unfeeling computer.

The results from an automatic might suffice for record shots but will always leave a lot to be desired aesthetically.

The semi-automatic is a step forward here, for there will be options left open to the user. An internal exposure meter is ready to do your bidding, and invariably there will be a choice, namely:

(a) fixed aperture and automatic exposure, or

(b) fixed exposure and automatic aperture.

The former of these two choices is the usual, as presetting of the iris controls the *depth of field* and can be quite important. All the user must do in this case, is to compose, focus, and know that the automatics will do the rest.

Some of the more advanced SLR's will have a third selector position. This is usually marked "prog" and indicates that the camera will follow a series of optimally chosen algorithms.

Recourse to this option is rare, and inhibits the user, but can be vital in rapidly changing situations when time to compose is very short.

The most meaningful and educational camera design is the manual operation. Here, the internal exposure meter will measure the light availability, and the choice is yours, to select both iris and shutter independently. Of course, the internal exposure meter must be satisfied, and will signal the "OK" only when the combination chosen will produce a perfectly exposed picture.

These cameras have no computer capacity, and as the exposure system is rugged and electrical, the cameras will virtually last forever. Some models of this type or similar use an electric shutter, and should the battery fail, the camera becomes useless.

There is at least one exception to this, known to the writer, and that is the LEICA R6, which has a fully mechanical shutter, allowing the user to continue shooting with settings based on experience. In view of this, such cameras are eagerly sought after, for with care, they will enjoy an incredibly long service life.

Choosing Lenses. Select with care.

When describing lenses, the most frequently heard word is "standard". Standard focal length in the 35mm format, is 50mm, for medium format, say 120 size, it is 80mm, and for the half plate camera, the most usual is 150mm.

When offered new, the camera will invariably be displayed fitted with the standard lens, for this will be the flagship, and the customer will tend to judge the system by the performance of the offered combination.

Experience shews that operationally, the 50mm is not the most reached for lens, but the 35mm, with its wider eye, and the ability to embrace a more natural tableaux that is constantly viewed by the unassisted eye.

No two people are the same, however. We had a lady in our club who saw everything mentally as through a short telephoto, and persistently walked about with an 85mm lens fitted to her camera.

She was happy, as was the Treasurer, who fitted a 28mm rather wide, and never used anything else. The ability to change lenses, gives an enormous feeling of freedom, and after a lifetime of photography, I can look in my holdall and feel that there is nothing "out there" that will beat me. Some of the really long lenses cost a fortune, but a little gadget called an "Extender" will multiply a focal length by two, at the expense of two "stops" of speed.

A cautionary note here.

With most makes, lenses will vary, not a lot, but noticeable to a quality "fanatic". This characteristic became so obvious at one time, that a certain Camera Dealer in London was offering nominated camera lenses in three grades.

"Tier one" was carefully selected, "Tier two" were those not quite making the Tier one grade, and "Tier three" were the remainder.

Naturally, as there was labour involved in selection, the Tier one lenses were more expensive. Public complaints were few, but I think it was the manufacturers that had it stopped. Why should there be a detectable variation in lenses of the same pattern?

The phenomenon is known as production spread, and as nearly all lenses are assembled automatically, there must be limits either side of optimum, defining which are acceptable. This is particularly the case where lenses are manufactured in Japan.

Hand assembled lenses such as Leica are individually checked at several points during their manufacture, and finally manually optimised on completion. This perfectionist approach reflects in the price of Leica Products.

A word here on Zoom lenses. In theory a good idea, as they can substitute for two or three fixed types.

Regrettably, they tend to be rather slow, and as they may contain anything up to fifteen separate elements, unlikely to offer fixed lens quality.

There are one or two dramatic exceptions to this, most of course, being Leica.

A word on filters: Not *just glass*

When not in use, a lens should always be covered, for it is the removal of the inevitable bits of grit that do the damage. Naturally, a lens cap can be clipped over in storage, but in use, a filter is almost mandatory.

The choice for general use is the grade marked UVa, as this will cover the use of either black and white or colour films. There is a lot of cheap rubbish about, with attractive prices, but it must be appreciated that filters are not just plain glass, but pigmented glass planes. Having spent a sizeable sum on your favourite lens, it would be madness to cover it with a substandard filter.

Match the filter to the filter thread on your lens, and go for the B&W brand, if you are not able to find a filter made by your camera maker.

Filters for black and white "Effects" can be a rampage of fun. For instance, in consideration of pictorial drama, a yellow filter may be fitted, although this will slow the film by its "Filter factor". Usually, a factor of two or even one and a half will modestly lift the clouds into the picture.

For high drama a 4-factor orange will produce just that, whilst a six-factor red will simulate night time conditions. There is endless fun to be had in this area, and the effects with black and white film are only limited by your ingenuity.

The use of filters artistically, is an occupation on its own, and there are one or two leaflets about, issued by filter manufacturers. I keep a rather scruffy pocket guide on filers handy that I picked up free of charge, from Messrs. BDB of Luton. (Beds)

Although colour film is available to suit either daylight or "tungsten" light, it can be used in either situation by the use of colour conversion filters, light blue, or very pale red as appropriate. This allows one film to be used universally.

Film. Only the best will do.

Despite continuous and often cleverly contrived rumours presumably started by vested interest in the digital field, Analog (film) photography is by no means dead.

Sales analysis shew that film sales are on the "up", and Kodak recently announced a new high-speed black and white film. There have been tragedies of course, and two of the finest films in the World, namely Kodachrome (colour) and Technical Pan (B/W). Have quietly slipped away. Both these moves were instigated by the modern "bottom line" philosophy.

In black and white, two long term stalwarts hold the fort, namely Ilford Ltd. and Kodak. Countless other films exist, many with curious names, but there is little doubt that these two leading brands hold the day. Ilford Ltd, using the Delta crystal technique, produce the Delta 100 (100ASA), film to challenge the popular Kodak equivalent, 100T.max.

Ilford offer higher speeds with their Delta technique, and details of the new high-speed Kodak film to be designated P3200Tmax is awaited.

Using standard manufacturing techniques, Kodak 400Tri-X is very popular with students.

In black and white, one must weigh up the performance advantages and disadvantages. The faster the film, the larger the *grain*, (the microscopic crystals forming the developed image).

The acuity of the film is also affected by the speed, thus the slower the film, the greater will be the *acuity*, or sharpness. Start with a good film, at say 100ASA, and stick with it. One can get adventurous later!

Colour films must be divided into two types. Colour print films and Colour positive (slide) films.

Colour print films are negative films and are printed very much in the same way as black and white, except of course the chemistry is different.

Perhaps a score of different types has passed through my hands, and in review, there is in my opinion, only one colour print film that stands out above the rest.

Fuji make a 200ASA colour print film that is just the right speed, is easy to use, and produces quite sharp images. Rightfully named "Superior" it has recently become difficult to find, but there are assurances that it will be replaced with a reliable alternative of the same speed.

A word of caution here. A good, well exposed film can be ruined by shoddy processing. The days of "popping" down to the local Chemist have long since gone, but there are one or two outstanding processors that fill the bill.

A popular long-established Darkroom can be found in Cheltenham, and they have had my colour work for years with never a complaint.

Colour slide films provide the maximum *acuity*, and in the days of Kodachrome, I have seen 35mm Kodachrome slides blown up to the size of the side of a house with breathtaking crispness.

When Kodachrome bowed out, Fuji jumped in to fill the bill with their Velvia and Provia ranges. Both these are rather costly but suit different tastes for natural hues and colour saturation.

There is an odd thing here that Fuji Velvia 100 is available wrapped in an AGFA pack, and sold as Precista CT100. The film is still made by Fuji, but purchased from Agfa, it is little more than half the price.

Beginners Guide to Analog (film) Photography

The whole market in films and cameras is rather like a bubbling cauldron, and it is a wise idea to have a handy "book of words" beside you.

A firm at Taunton trading under the name "First call" do an excellent catalogue, covering the whole spectrum of amateur photography activity. This is £7.99 separately but is free with your first purchase. This catalogue can guide the beginner far more reliably that a monthly magazine.

Watch out for the few outlets of discount films online who will supply directly, enabling substantial thrift in the early stages, these firms usually offer films in packs of five, resulting in substantial savings.

Getting at it: The World is your oyster.

A pivotal point in family life is the arrival of a new member and as we now have with us a film camera, which is more accurate and detailed than any pocket notebook, we can record the events as they happen.

In a way, such thoughts triggered off the generation of this booklet, as indicated in the introduction.

Photographing babies in the hands of a loving mother is easy to capture, but a word of warning here. If the light available is poor, and you wish to use flash, never, on any account, shoot flash into babies face until at least six weeks of age, and probably more.

When short of light, and it is not possible to use daylight, set *the lens iris two stops wider*, and bounce the flash off the ceiling.

Usually this proves to be quite satisfactory, but remember, once finished with bouncing, return the lens to the iris setting recommended on the back of the flash gun.

If your flash unit is mounted inside the camera body, ensure the flash is switched "off" and use either room lighting or daylight, say near a window.

In these circumstances, the shutter speed required may be longer than usual, so a steady touch is required.

A methodical recording of "junior's" progress is a joy in itself, but my Family Album starts with a photo of my father in uniform in 1917, and is still being added to, to this day. Some shots are a trifle scruffy, but are still in good shape, safe, not in the least vulnerable, and are mine.

Let us open our minds, and stroll away, always on the lookout for inviting shots. Records are up to date, and the family album is filling nicely, so we can now use our imagination and start looking for more interesting shots, that should ideally carry a message.

A good point here is to clear up a couple of schoolboy howlers. The first is fairly obvious, but in the heat of the moment can be easily overlooked. *Never get the sun in the picture!*

You have given the camera a quandary here, for the built-in exposure system will detect the sun, and shut down the exposure system to cope. This will leave your subject in the deepest of gloom.

With a semi-automatic system, the camera may be twisted until the sun is out of the frame, accordingly, the iris is then set to the new required setting. The camera may now be returned to the original composition and the exposure made.

Obviously, one must ignore the complaints from the exposure system, but you will at least have a picture. By far the best approach is to adjust your position such that the sun is out of the frame.

Just a little is enough, for lens hoods are very good. (Cameras advanced enough to offer a "memory lock" facility, have this problem well covered. In practice, merely by looking away from the problem sun in the composition, taking first pressure on the release, will lock the setting, and allow that setting to be used when the final release is pressed.)

The second howler is immediately obvious whilst using an SLR but might be missed in a minor way when using a pocket automatic. The difficulty revolves around using a wide-angle lens in close-up, for it can introduce distortion by inordinately enlarging a part of the target nearest to the camera compared with the remainder.

The classic howler is to photograph your subject, perhaps lying down, feet towards you. The result can be hilarious, but a lesson to be learned just the once.

As the family grow, they will be duly recorded. No need to bore your friends with these, but use chances to exploit situations, that can really make the shot stand out.

My son and I were at an air display, and I decided to stand him beside the landing wheel of a Vulcan bomber. His diminutive figure beside the gaping air intakes was such a contrast, the effect was magic...

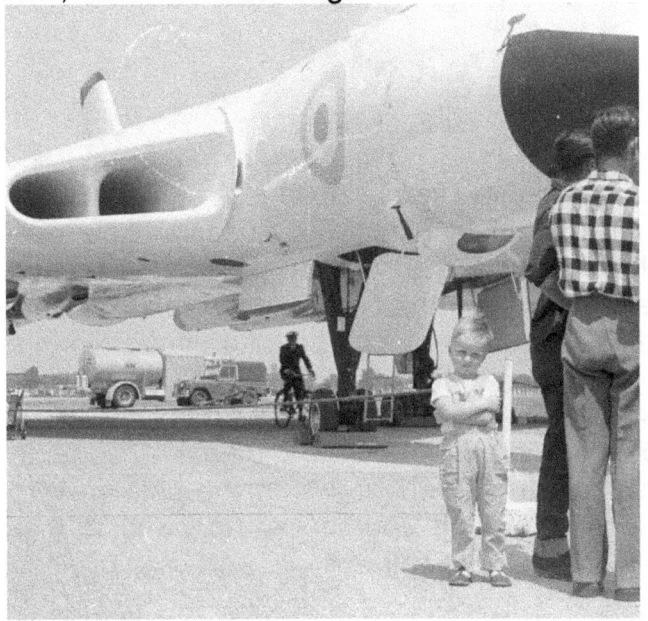

Being a keen cyclist, I had an arrangement whereby I was able to carry the camera wherever I go, and invested in a *"Handlebar Bag"*

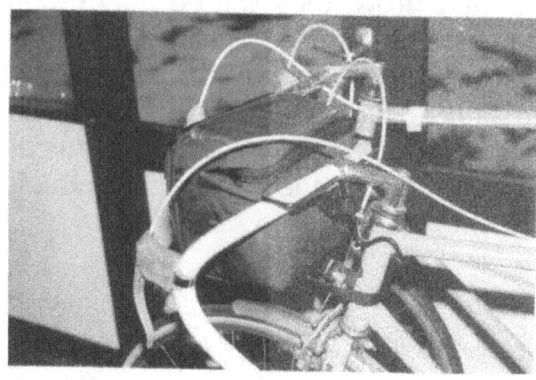

which can sit quite safely between the bends of the racing type handlebar. Instant readiness is the need of course, and for a couple of years, this worked reasonably effectively, although even the time needed to stop, zip open the bag, and use the camera, can be long enough to miss an unexpected deer, or magnificent moment.

The answer was a chest harness and a holster.

This sounds terrible, but when adjusted correctly, is perfect. The camera sits lens down in the holster, with the neck strap loosely around your neck. No need to "Velcro" down the tab, the camera will not fall, and you are instantly ready.

On no account try to cycle with a camera slung loosely around your neck for it will damage both the camera and your health. It will catch in everything, and disaster will result, and you might even finish up in the hedge!

Incidentally, the handlebar bag had proved so useful as a platform for my route maps, it was retained, and used as storage for spare lenses and film.

Cycling is magic for catching the right pics. Walking is good, but too slow whilst on the lookout. Cycling can take you from place to place quite quickly, you have no parking problems, so can stop almost instantly to browse, park quietly, and find an optimum position to shoot.

Seaside shots in England are post carded in every shop you visit, but with a touch of sly cunning, it is possible to capture an artful twist to the scene and make that shot a winner.

By using *differential focusing*, the background of the shot just identifies the resort, but the focal point is the capstan of course.

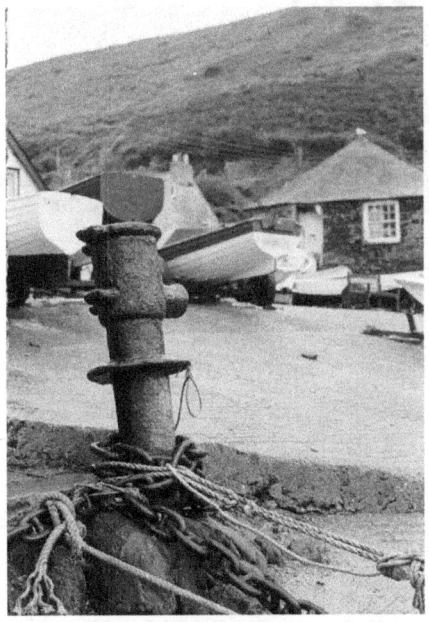

What a tale that could tell, with the wide assortment of tether ropes accumulated over the years.

The further north one travels, captivating scenes are in abundance, but tarry a moment in Cornwall...

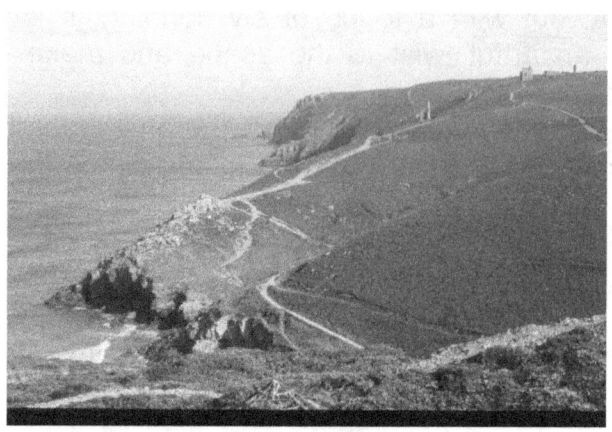

Here we have a high vantage point, and some sea line. Ensure that this is horizontal! Note details of the coastal walk, and mining ruins.

Scotland by cycle (or any other means, come to that) is an absolute gold mine, and dozens of little nuggets can be wrinkled out with patience.

Landscapes surround in abundance. Tours in the highlands area revealed many moving vistas

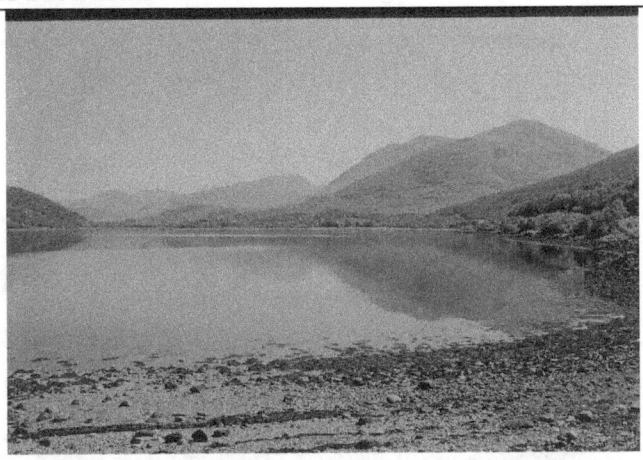

Loch Creran is a stretch of water, perhaps a mile in diameter, skirted on all sides by mountain slopes, right down to the waters level.

My cycle and I were privileged to find a gap to view. The Sun above and summer clouds did not apply here.

The silence was so complete, it seemed to put an unexpected pressure on the ears. *There was no birdsong*, but a just perceptible lapping sound of the water's edge against the pebbles at my feet. This sombre almost menacing bulk of high ground made this one of my greatest challenges to record the mood.

Being an Engineer, my technical tours were frequent, mainly aviation and locomotion displays. However, once the routine records had been taken, one looks for a captivating shot, and the shot below is just that...

Beginners Guide to Analog (film) Photography

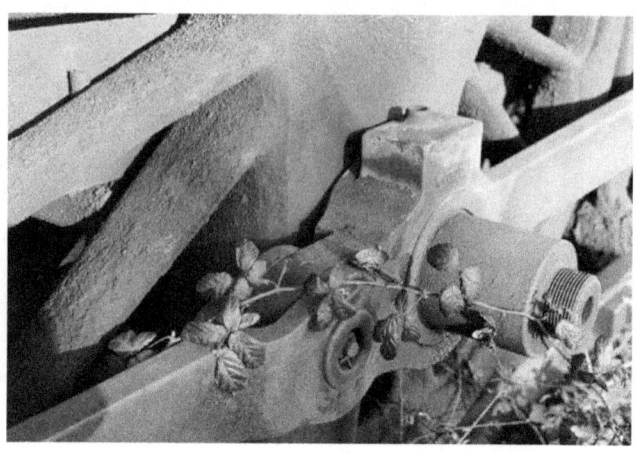

This is the saddest of twists, for it was taken in a locomotive graveyard! I called this *Loco:0, - Nature 1!*

On a lighter note: Humour magazines and comics are always on the lookout for clever bursts of harmless humour.

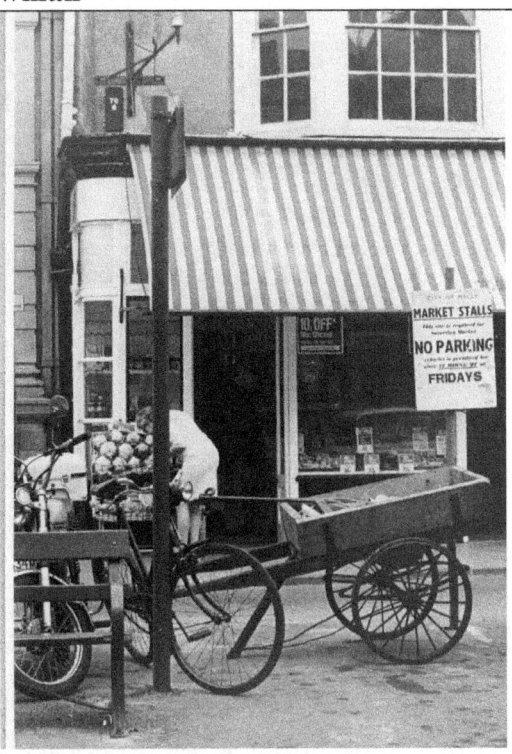

This shot, taken near Wells Cathedral took my fancy, representing what I took to be an impish challenge to Ecclesiastic Authority.

As the years go by, the photography of our beautiful buildings in this Country becomes increasingly difficult. In earlier days, the presence of telegraph wires was a problem, then it became television antennas, now of course, it is both these plus the ubiquitous nose to tail parking of cars.

The magnificent timbered offices in the centre of Gloucester deserved to have a great deal of attention.

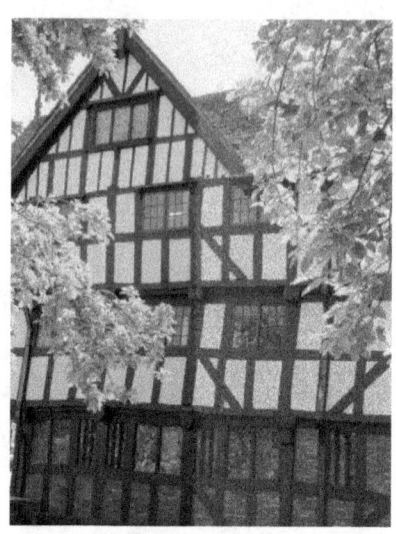

By taking two or three circulatory trips around the building with various lens options, it was possible to invoke the help of surrounding trees, and virtually eliminate all the modern clutter.

Leaving my pet subject of thatched and timbered cottages, it is possible to move into the grounds of stately homes, and hope for freedom from these impedimenta.

The construction of these homes is often massive, and a plain record shot will have no appeal. Pick out a little oddity and concentrate on that. In cases where the buildings, are particularly plain, find some nearby trees, move under an overhanging branch, and adjust your position until the foliage frames the building.

This old adage can sometimes yield positive results. (Gloucester above, is the typical technique.)

Overseas travel: Even before you start, (and if, by now you consider yourself an enthusiastic photographer). Prepare your trip with precision.

Study precisely where you are going, even listing well known buildings, and plan carefully. If this is not done, immediately upon arrival, you will suffer from *photographic saturation.* Everyone makes this error just once, and a high order of self-discipline is required.

All the usual rules still apply, but of course, one is surrounded by an enormous number of temptations, and running short of film can result.

Hold the camera to your eye, with the finger away from the shutter, and look at the scene, move to either side, even back and forth until the composition pleases. Only then press the shutter release.

The result will give satisfaction, and there has been no waste.

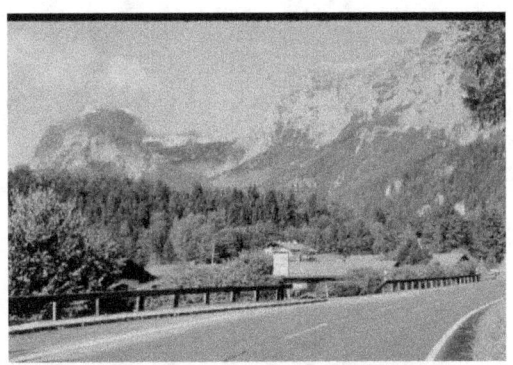

Surely this must be Bavaria!

An important point here associated with overseas travel, is to ensure that you have your film in one of the thin lead bags now available, to protect your film from the X-ray tests on your person and baggage.

Now and again, a situation may occur where there has been no time to prepare, and you find yourself in the midst of a strange town or village.

The well-trodden path is to make your way to a local curio/antique shop and look in the window for the usual collection of etchings of the village. Here, all your homework is done for you, and the system can be exploited to the full.

To finish on an amusing note. The shot of my Daughter in the introduction is entitled "Little Madam" This "goodbye" shot is entitled "Modern Madam".

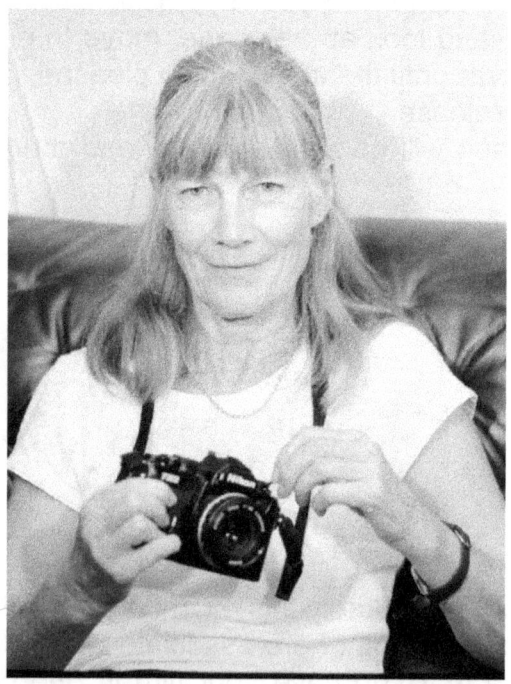

The two shots are fifty-four years apart, and both look as though they had been taken yesterday. *Using analog photography.*

John. Plowman.

About the Author

John A Plowman was born in Luton, Bedfordshire on June 13th, 1924, son of Tom Plowman, later of motor racing fame.

John was educated at Dunstable School Bedfordshire, and then on to the University College of North Wales, Bangor, specialising in Radio and Electrical Engineering.

Drafted into the Aircraft industry during the war years, John stayed with aviation on his return after three years in the RAF, retiring in 1985, from Westland Helicopters. (Yeovil), as C.Eng. MIET.

Although devoted to aviation, there has always been two substantial hobbies in his life, namely Model Engineering and Photography.

As you will glean from this little booklet, John has resisted most of the digital advances in photo techniques and is still able to follow the original path of Film Photography, proudly showing his first efforts in portraiture, taken in April 1941.

The return to analogue photography is currently manifest World Wide, and the writer hopes this this tiny contribution has helped.

Frequently Used Terms Explained:

Some terminology used in this book may be unfamiliar, so an easy explanation for these is listed below. Where such expressions appear for the first time in the text, they will be printed in *italics,* and will appear in the list below.

ASA: The *speed rating* of the film in use. ASA stands for American Standards Association. Remember, the larger the number. The more sensitive the film.

DIN: The equivalent to ASA but now barely used in Europe, as these ratings are logarithmic and not linear as in ASA, terrible confusion will be caused. Ignore reference to DIN on film packets, and very old European camera bodies.

Aperture scale, aperture, f/stop: Ways of indicating the speed of a lens, which is controlled by the diameter of the *iris* (the hole through which the light must pass). Lenses are rated at their *full aperture* (largest hole available), usually expressed as the Ratio of the focal length divided by the maximum iris diameter, thus: 50mm/f/2. The iris control is invariably in *click stops*, each stop representing a halving of the iris area., not diameter.

Stopping down, opening up: Opening up refers to the iris area being increased, and vice versa. See *click stops above.*

Focal length. Usually expressed in millimeters, although with some very early English designs, you will find this expressed in inches. The focal length is the distance between the back of the lens and the face of the film, when the lens is set to infinity. There are exceptions to this, namely retrofocus lenses, described elsewhere.

Depth of field: The distance between two points in view that will provide adequate appearance of sharpness. Stopping down will increase depth of field, and in some settings, out beyond "infinity"

"Reach" A more recent phraseology, quite an arbitrary parameter suggesting the distance at which the coverage of the lens will represent a more normal perspective in the viewfinder. A telephoto lens will be described as having more *reach,* increasing, as the focal length is increased.

Over Exposure. The result of maladjustment of settings resulting in too much light reaching the film. The negative will usually have jet black skies (sometime known as blocked skies). Deep shadow may print out, but most other detail is lost. There is a chemical treatment that can partially remedy this situation (in B/W) to dissolve some of the densest image.

Under Exposure. A maladjustment of settings resulting in too little light reaching the film. Often skies will print in (just), but most of the other detail is too "thin" to print. There is available a process of "intensification" of the image, but this is rarely acceptable.

Contrast. The ratio between the densest and the lightest part of the image. The ASA settings advised on all films will provide what is accepted as "normal" contrast. For special effects (sometimes referred to as "FX"), it is possible to expose the film quite outside its ratings. This is called *"pushing"* (over rating), and *"pulling"* (under rating). The lab must be advised of this, otherwise they are not able to chemically compensate for the technique.

Plate, Half plate, Quarter plate. Originally used to describe the size of the photo plate in use. Nowadays the sizes are confined to describing the size of the print. In the thirties, quarter plate prints were usually supplied by the labs, or your local chemist. Since the War, a larger format has been adopted. This lies between quarter and half plate and is the popular 6"x4". The whole plate is replaced by readily available 7"X5". There are commercial reasons for this change.

Freedom. Another quite arbitrary saying that has crept into photographic parlance. This describes a wonderful situation, where a combination of film speed, and brilliant sunshine renders the advantage of the iris to be well stopped down yet have plenty of shutter speed in hand. Occasionally used to describe a lens offering the advantage of extremely high speed.